STANLEY THORNES
PRIMARY

Literacy

Textbook

YEAR
5

Lydia Fulleylove

First published by

Stanley Thornes Publishers Ltd
Ellenborough House
Wellington Street
Cheltenham
GL50 1YW

.
00 01 02 03 04 \ 10 9 8 7 6 5 4 3 2

A catalogue record for this book is available from the British Library

ISBN 0-7487-4825-3

Illustrations © STP, by:

Dick Barton, Louise Barton, Ron Bell, Claire Boyce, Anna Cattermole, Debbie Clarke, Joan Corlass, Beverley Curl, Jacqueline East, Serena Feneziani, Jane Gerwitz, Diana Gold, Michelle Ives, Karen Kett, Jean de Lemos, Mandy Lillywhite, Tony O'Donnell, Mike Pell, Zara Slattery, Margaret Theakston, Kirsty Wilson

Design by Oxford Designers and Illustrators/ STP.
Page make up by Aetos Ltd, Bathampton, Bath.
Printed and bound in Italy
by G. Canale & C.S.p.A., Borgaro T .se, Turin.

Contents

The Haunted Lighthouse

Activity 1

You will need the Anthology, Resource Sheet 1 and your writing materials.

Work quietly on your own. Read the questions on the Resource Sheet. Then reread the extract before you write the answers carefully in sentences.

Activity 2

You will need the Anthology and your writing materials.

Start by talking in your group about what you think will happen next. Then work on your own and write three or four sentences which carry on the story. Read the last three paragraphs first. Check your work carefully, then read your idea aloud to the group.

Support: work through Resource Sheet 2 on speech marks.

Activity 3

You will need the Anthology and your writing materials.

Imagine that you are Philip. Think about what he is feeling as he stands alone at the top of the lighthouse at the beginning of the story. Then write three or four sentences as if you were Philip. You could use the sentence below to start:

It's so lonely up here.

Extension: rewrite the story from the point of view of one of the seals. You will need to think about why the seals are there and what they know. Remember to proofread and check your writing.

Activity 4

You will need the Anthology and your writing/drawing materials.

In your group read aloud the first three paragraphs. Discuss the picture it makes you see. Then work on your own to draw a picture which fits the words closely. Write a sentence which expresses what Philip might have said if he had spoken his thoughts aloud. Remember to use speech marks, for example, "What can they be doing?" wondered Philip.

Activity 5

You will need the Anthology and your writing materials.

You are going to decide whether you would like to read more of the story, and why. Try to include comments on these points:

- the main character
- the beginning
- exciting or interesting points
- any especially striking words or phrases.

When you have finished, read your work to make sure it is clear, and check the spellings. You may find it helpful to read your review aloud to a partner in your group.

Here Comes Charlie Moon

Activity 1

You will need the Anthology and your writing/drawing materials.

Reread the story quietly together then work on your own.

Choose one character, either Charlie or Ariadne. Write down the name of the character you choose, what you know about that character and how he or she behaves. If you have time, draw and label your character. Remember to check your work carefully.

Activity 2

You will need the Anthology, Resource Sheet 3 and your writing materials.

Read the passage on the Resource Sheet which is taken from the beginning of the story. You are going to think of a word to fit each space. You don't have to remember the words in the story. There are often several possible words.

When you have written a word in each space read the whole passage again to check it makes sense. Then read through the passage together, discussing the words you all chose, and decide which fits best. Finally, compare what you have written with the original paragraph.

Activity 3

You will need the Anthology and your writing materials.

Read the extract again silently. Think about what you know about the characters, the storyline and the setting so far. Then write the next five sentences of the story. Remember to use the same tense as in the extract. Check your work carefully, then read it aloud to a partner or the group.

Activity 4

You will need the Anthology and drawing materials.

Reread the first paragraph of the story. Each person in your group should say one thing he or she has learned about the shop. Then on your own, draw the inside of the shop. You can draw the outside as well if you have time. Make sure your drawing matches the details given in the text and give it a title.

Activity 5

You will need the Anthology, Resource Sheet 4 and your writing materials.

Reread the part where Charlie chases the thieves. Use the Resource Sheet to help you to write two paragraphs describing an exciting chase. Think carefully about what verbs you are going to use. Think of a title for your writing.

Activity 6

You will need the Anthology and your writing/drawing materials.

Write about the character you would most like to be. Write about the sort of person he or she is and say why you would choose this character. Draw and label a picture to illustrate your work if you have time.

Activity 7

You will need the Anthology and your writing materials.

Write another episode of the story. You should invent one new character. Look back at the text to make sure that your episode follows on from what you already know.

Be Safe Outdoors

Activity 1

You will need the Anthology, Resource Sheet 5 and your writing materials.

You are going to use Resource Sheet 5 to help you write a set of instructions for a task or activity that you know well. Start by rereading the project instructions in the Anthology. Then decide how you will fit your instructions into the frame. Remember that the correct order is important. Read them out to your group to see if they are clear.

Extension: you are going to write a set of rules for a game you know or have invented, or you could try writing your own set of school rules.

draw up board

draw figure and colour

fold tab

leave tab on feet

glue on to base

Activity 2

You will need the Anthology, Resource Sheet 5 and your writing/drawing materials.

You are going to rewrite the section on dealing with sprains as a set of instructions. You should use Resource Sheet 5 to help you organise your points and add a picture to each point. Remember to use the imperative.

Example: first take off the shoe and raise the foot.

Activity 3

You will need the Anthology and your writing/drawing materials.

You are going to create a set of simple drawings with written instructions which tell you how to make something. These can be funny or serious, but they must be clear. The picture on page 23 of the Anthology may help you. Do not write more than five points and keep them simple.

Ideas: How to make a mud pie

            How to make a monster

Activity 4

You will need the Anthology and your writing materials.

Look carefully at the picture showing dangerous situations with your group. Discuss the dangers you can spot. Then work on your own and write a sentence about each danger. If there is time you could work with your group to make a list of dos and don'ts.

Example: don't play on railway lines.

Activity 5

You will need the Anthology and your writing/drawing materials.

You are going to design your own safety poster for the school playground. First look carefully at the introduction in the text, and the picture showing dangerous situations. Make a list of dangerous things which could happen in your school playground. These can be in note form to start with. Then sketch a picture to show some of these things happening in the playground. Try not to make them all too obvious, so that the reader has to look carefully at your poster.

Then write a clear list of dos and don'ts for safety in your school playground. Remember to use the imperative form.

Examples: Don't kick footballs near the windows.

Put all litter in the bins provided.

Poems (1)

Activity 1

You will need the Anthology, Resource Sheet 7 and your writing materials.

You are going to use the outline on Resource Sheet 7 to help you write your own poem about a real or imaginary special place. Start by rereading Jackie Kay's poem. Then think of your own place. Make sure you picture it in your mind before you start writing. When you have made your first draft you could read it aloud to a partner to help you see what may need changing. You may need extra time after the lesson to edit and proofread your work and make a final version. You will probably want to think of your own title.

Activity 2

You will need the Anthology, Resource Sheet 6 and your writing materials.

Use the Resource Sheet to help you jot down your thoughts about one of the poems you have read this week. You may want to highlight unusual or striking words, ask questions and say what you especially like or dislike about the poem. When you have finished share your thoughts with a partner or your group.

Activity 3

You will need the Anthology and drawing materials.

You are going to make a detailed drawing to illustrate one of the poems you have read this week. Reread it closely first to make sure you understand all the details. You will need to think carefully about how you will illustrate all the stanzas.

Activity 4

You will need the Anthology.

You are going to prepare a group presentation of one of the poems you have read this week. First reread it quietly on your own. Then discuss how you are going to present it as a group. Which parts will everyone read? Which lines could be read by one or two people? Do any parts need to be louder or softer? Faster or slower? Think about the mood of the poem and what sort of expression you can try to put into your voices. Look at the punctuation and any run-on lines and think about where you need to pause.

Activity 5

You will need copies of the poems you have read this week, Resource Sheets 6 and 8 and your writing materials.

Decide which poem is your favourite. You are going to write about why you like this poem. Try to include several different points, using Resource Sheet 6 to help you. For example:

- the look on the page

- sounds and rhymes

- rhythm

- message

- mood or atmosphere

- any unusual or striking lines.

Make clear your reasons for choosing this poem. Check your work carefully and read it aloud to a partner or the group.

Extension: use the outline on Resource Sheet 8 to create your own message poem.

Sabre-tooth Sandwich

Activity 1

You will need the Anthology, Resource Sheet 9 and your writing materials. Work quietly on your own to answer the questions.

Activity 2

You will need the Anthology, Resource Sheet 10 and your writing materials.

Read Chapter One quietly on your own. You are going to see how much you can find out about uncle's character. Then complete the two lists on the Resource Sheet. One will contain facts about uncle and the other will contain other people's opinions of uncle.

Then draw a picture of uncle, using the last three paragraphs of the chapter to help you.

Activity 3

You will need your writing materials.

When we describe one thing by comparing it to another we call it a simile.

Here are some examples:

My father scowls like a thunder sky.
The sun went down as red and angry as my father's face.

Now make up your own similes to describe the angry father and uncle's loud voice.

Example:

My father was as angry as an injured lion.
My uncle's voice was as loud as a giant's roar.

Work on your own to write your similes. Then read your similes aloud to the group. Help each other rewrite them to make them as interesting as possible. Carefully write out your best simile.

Activity 4

You will need the Anthology and your writing materials.

You are going to rewrite reported speech as direct speech. Here is an example of reported speech from the story:

> My father says he is a lazy, no good layabout and if he wasn't my mother's brother, he'd be out of our cave faster than smoke.

Here is the same speech written as direct speech:

> "You're a lazy no-good layabout and if you weren't my wife's brother, you'd be out of this cave faster than smoke," said my father.

or

> "He's a lazy no-good layabout and if he wasn't my wife's brother, he'd be out of this cave faster than smoke," said my father.

Read the examples of reported speech which are at the top of page 20. Work on your own and write each one as direct speech. Remember to use speech marks to show the words that are being spoken and the correct punctuation inside the speech marks. Then take it in turns to read each speech aloud to the group. Notice which words you have needed to change.

We live, says my uncle, at the dawn of history and are really quite primitive.

My father mutters under his breath that he had something more substantial than a finger in mind.

Just because we live at the dawn of history, he says, there's no need to go about looking as if we've just got out of bed.

Extension: write an additional scene from the point of view of any member of the family. Use the first person and think about what the character you have chosen is feeling. Experiment with short sentences to create suspense. You might want to use the following points to give shape to your narrative.

The character is alone in the forest when a strange beast approaches.

What does the character do?

Activity 5

You will need the Anthology and your writing materials.

You are going to record your thoughts and opinions about the story. Remember that it is important to refer to the text to support your comments. Sometimes you may want to use words from the text, for example, to describe a character. The outline below may help you to structure your writing.

You could include:

- a few sentences about the storyline

- comments on the main characters

- what you think the writer's message might be

- what you liked best or least about the story and why

- whether or not you would like to read another book by this author and why/why not.

Check your work carefully. Add extra pieces to make the meaning clear and delete any words you don't need. Proofread and make a final version. It sometimes helps to ask a partner to read through your work. Reading your work backwards is often useful when you are checking for spelling mistakes.

Wood

Activity 1

You will need the Anthology, Resource Sheet 11 and your writing materials.

Work with a partner. Think of three or four questions which the text may help you to answer. Using Resource Sheet 11, write these questions in the first column. Then find the answers in the text and write them in the second column. If you can find any extra details write them in the third column. Write the title of the extract and the author in the fourth column. If you have time write your information clearly in sentences. Think of a title for your work.

Activity 2

You will need Resource Sheet 12 and your writing materials.

You are going to skim and scan the text to find the answers to the questions on Resource Sheet 12. Write the answers carefully, using full stops and capital letters. Check spellings when you have finished.

Activity 3

You will need a dictionary and your writing materials.

You are going to make a list of words that end in "ist". Use a dictionary to check the meaning of words you don't know. Give your list a heading, for example, "Occupation words", and write the words and their definitions.

Activity 4

You will need the Anthology and your writing materials.

Look carefully at one of the pictures. Remember that pictures can tell you as much as, or more than words. Choose four or five things which you learn from the picture. Write a sentence about each.

Activity 5

You will need the Anthology, Resource Sheet 13, the work you have done this week and your writing materials.

Using Resource Sheet 13, you are going to organise some of the information you have found. Look at the text and the work you have done during the week to help you to decide what you want to record. Then write this information clearly and neatly using the guide sentences on the Resource Sheet. Make up your own title.

Check your work carefully and read it aloud to your partner.

Extension: add your own sentences to the ones suggested on the Resource Sheet.

Or

Think of your own way of organising and presenting the information. This might be a poster, a report or a piece of imaginative writing based on the facts, as in the one about the ghost which you did with the class.

Bill's New Frock

Activity 1

You will need your writing materials.

Write two paragraphs about a dream in which people you know treat you differently in some way. What do you feel? What do you learn? If you are stuck you may find Resource Sheet 14 helpful.

Activity 2

You will need the Anthology, a dictionary and your writing materials.

You are going to rewrite the opening speech as if you are a girl who has turned into a boy. Try to show what she is feeling. Read the opening speech again, but try not to copy it. You can discuss what she might say with your group, but work on your own to write the speech. Your speech should be set out just like Bill's.

Activity 3

You will need the Anthology, Resource Sheet 15 and your writing materials.

You are going to turn a piece of script back into direct speech. Start with "Up you get ..." and finish with "I'm late for work".

Think carefully about the rules of direct speech before you start.

Activity 4

You will need the Anthology. You will be working with your group.

You are going to read aloud the scene you have just studied. Think about what your character is like and what he or she is feeling and try to show this in your voice. You also need to think about where you need to pause. Decide who will read each part. Read the scene several times giving different people a turn at different parts if you need to.

Activity 5

Discuss with your group a scene about a girl who turns into a boy for the day. Where is she? What happens? Who is she with? What does she feel? Then act out this scene. Make sure there are enough parts for everyone. Try to begin and end with a "still picture". Practise it and present it to the class.

Activity 6

You will need your writing materials.

Discuss a scene where a girl turns into a boy for the day. Where is she? Who is with her? What happens? How does she feel? Can you make your scene begin and end in an especially interesting/dramatic way?

Work together and write a script for this scene. You should each make your own copy. Read it aloud, then check and edit it.

Activity 7

You will need the Anthology, Resource Sheet 16 and your writing materials.

You are going to evaluate the script. Use the points on the Resource Sheet to help you comment. You may want to add your own comments as well.

What was it about? If you have read the novel, how was the play script different? What do you think of the beginning? The ending? Which character would you like to act? Which character would you not like to act?

Check your work and share it with a partner.

The Dead Letter Box

Activity 1

You will need the Anthology and your writing materials.

You are going to write an extract from either Glenda's or Louie's diary. You should base this on the section you have read today. You should record what happens and show the character's feelings. You might find it helpful to discuss the two characters with your group first, commenting on how they are different. Then work on your own. Remember to use the first person in your writing. Leave yourself time to review and proofread your work before reading it aloud to the group.

Activity 2

You will need the Anthology and your writing materials.

You are going to predict what happens next. You should include a short conversation between Louie and Glenda which uses direct speech. Before you start writing, reread the last few paragraphs of the section you have read today and discuss your ideas with your group.

You should concentrate on making your writing clear and interesting. Leave yourself time to review and proofread your work before you read it aloud to the group.

Activity 3

You will need the Anthology, Resource Sheet 17 and your writing materials.

You are going to choose a short section of dialogue from the story and turn it into script. You should choose the section together and discuss what to write together. You should each write a script of your own. You can use Resource Sheet 17 to help you if you wish. Include directions for the actors if you need to. Look at the example below to remind yourself how to set out a script. Check your script carefully, then read it aloud with the group.

Example:

GLENDA: You got finished quickly. *(surprised)*

LOUIE: I wanted to talk to you. When are you moving?

Activity 4

You will need the Anthology and your writing/drawing materials.

You are going to make a drawing which fits the text closely and which shows you have noticed the details. Your drawing should include a character with a thought bubble. You should give the drawing a title. You should choose from the examples below. Do not include a drawing for a section you have not yet read.

1. Draw a picture to fit the first two paragraphs of the story.

2. Draw a picture to show Louie and Glenda in the library. You can include a thought bubble for each character for this one.

3. Draw a picture to show Louie in the children's library.

Extension: imagine you are Louie or Glenda and write an account of a dream or nightmare. Remember to write in the first person.

Activity 5

You will need the Anthology and your writing materials.

You are going to write Louie's first letter to Glenda. Before you start, think carefully about all you know about both characters and look back at the text to check details. Include one special thing that Louie would like Glenda to do. Think carefully about how to end your letter.

Activity 6

You will need the Anthology, Resource Sheet 18 and your writing materials.

You are going to write an evaluation to show what you think of this story. You can include good and bad points. Use Resource Sheet 18, but try to write down your own thoughts and questions as well.

Concrete Poems

Activity 1

You will need the Anthology, Resource Sheet 19 and your writing materials.

Read two or three examples of shape poems from the Anthology. Notice how their shapes fit their subjects. Then look at the examples on the Resource Sheet. Make your own poems to fit these shapes.

Extension: you are going to write a shape poem about a feeling which is connected with an activity – for example, the feeling of excitement may be connected with the activity of opening a parcel. Think of some words which express the feeling and then try some different ways of arranging them on the page. When you are ready, edit and proofread your work and show it to a partner. You can think of your own ideas for the poems, or use one of the ideas below:

feeling hot – a melting ice-cream cone

feeling cold – words and letters jumping about like teeth chattering

feeling happy – a smiling face.

Activity 2

You will need the Anthology, Resource Sheet 6 and your writing materials.

Read aloud the poems from today's lesson. Discuss similarities and differences between them and which one you prefer and why. Then use the Resource Sheet to help you write a paragraph about one of the poems. Finish by saying what you like or dislike about this poem and give your reasons. Check your work and read it aloud to your group.

Extension: find more examples of concrete poems in other anthologies and poetry books, and discuss them. Compare them with the ones you have read in the lesson.

Activity 3

You will need the Anthology.

Work in pairs. Choose one of the poems from today's lesson and prepare a reading of this poem with your partner. Look carefully at the punctuation and think about where to pause. Think about the mood of the poem and how you can change your voice by varying the pace, the pitch and the volume. Decide which lines you could read together. When you have practised, present your poem to the group.

Activity 4

You will need the Anthology and your writing/drawing materials.

Reread the poem "Daddy fell into the pond". Think about the picture which it gives you, then choose one stanza. Identify what each line makes you see and then make a drawing which fits this stanza closely. Give your drawing a title.

Activity 5

You will need the Anthology, Resource Sheet 6 and your writing materials.

Look at the poems you have read this week, and decide which two you like best. Write a paragraph about each poem, saying what you like and why. Justify your views with reference to the text. You may find Resource Sheet 6 helpful. You should edit and proofread your work and share it with your group.

Nelson Mandela

Activity 1

You will need the Anthology, Resource Sheet 20 and your writing materials.

You should work on your own. Use the frame on the Resource Sheet to help you record what you already know about Nelson Mandela and what you would like to know. Use the last box to record some important things you have found out. You may want to add a few sentences of your own to your account. Check your work carefully before reading it to the group.

Activity 2

You will need the Anthology, Resource Sheet 21 and your writing materials.

You are going to imagine that you are Nelson Mandela in one of the pictures. Spend a few minutes discussing the pictures with your group, then work on your own. Use the first person and write down what you might be thinking. If you have read the section entitled "Long years in jail", you could choose the picture of Nelson in jail and use the information in the text to help you write a diary extract for Nelson. Check your work and read it to your group.

Activity 3

You will need the Anthology and your writing materials.

Choose two pictures from the section you have just read. Look carefully at the details and then write five facts which you learn from the pictures. You can also add some questions about each picture. Check your work before reading it aloud to your group.

Activity 4

You will need the Anthology and your writing materials.

You are going to choose five of the words which are written in bold in the text. Use the glossary at the back to find the meanings. Then write one sentence for each word. For example: Lawyer: the lawyer said that the man would be found guilty.

Activity 5

You will need Resource Sheet 22 and your writing materials.

You are going to write a recount of a visit, an event or a personal experience. Use Resource Sheet 22 to organise your work.

You may then want to write in more detail without the frame. Think about these points as you organise your writing:

- chronological order – words to connect your writing, for example, "after that".

- paragraphs – you may want to start a new paragraph for each main point.

Read your work aloud to a partner and then produce a neat, accurate final version.

Blitz

Activity 1

You will need the Anthology and your writing materials.

You are going to write a paragraph to open a story in which the place is especially important. Look carefully at the way the wood piles are described as a city in the text and then use your imagination in a similar way about a place which you know. For example, a tree-house could be a raft at sea, a tumbledown shack could be a cave, an airing cupboard could be a ...? Spend a few moments talking about your idea with your group and listening to their ideas, then work on your own to draft a paragraph. When you have finished check your work and read it aloud to the group.

Activity 2

You will need the Anthology, Resource Sheet 23 and your writing materials.

You are going to start a reading log to record your thoughts about the story so far. Try to include comments on:

- what you know about the characters

- the opening – does it make you want to read on?

- any striking words or phrases.

You may want to use Resource Sheet 23 to organise your writing. Check your work carefully and then read it aloud to the group.

Activity 3

You will need Resource Sheet 24 and your writing/drawing materials.

You are going to draw a map or a picture to show the ruined city of Kor. Read the paragraphs describing the city carefully. Use Resource Sheet 24 to highlight details which you think you will use in your picture. Write a sentence about the city to go with your picture.

Activity 4

You will need the Anthology, Resource Sheet 25 and your writing materials.

You are going to make a list of questions about the story. You should include anything you don't understand and are curious about, as well as any words whose meaning you are not sure of. If you have time, look the words up in a dictionary. Finally, write a sentence predicting what will happen next. Your sentence should start "I think that ...".

Use Resource Sheet 25 to help you.

Extension: write your own ending for the story. Remember to read the last few paragraphs of the extract and think about what might happen to the boys and the pilot.

Activity 5

You will need the Anthology and your writing materials.

Work with a partner. Choose one of the scenes below. If you decide on the scene from the text, read it carefully. You are going to act out this scene, showing what the boys are feeling through what they say and the way they move. You should begin and end your scene with a "freeze frame" (still picture).

Practise the scene several times until you are confident of what you are saying and doing, then present it to the group.

1. Show the scene where the boys edge up to the plane and then discover the pilot is alive.

Or

2. Devise your own scene where you force yourself to do something frightening.

Extension: discuss or think about any one of these scenes and then write a script for it.

The Iron Woman

Activity 1

You will need the Anthology, Resource Sheet 23 and your writing materials.

You are going to record your thoughts and impressions of the story so far. This is called a reading log and it is a useful way of keeping track of your thoughts about a story.

You may want to use Resource Sheet 23 to help you organise your writing. Check your work and read it aloud to your group.

Activity 2

You will need the Anthology and your writing materials.

You are going to write your own blurb for a book you know well. Reread the blurb for *The Iron Woman* first.

Points to remember:

- use the present tense
- include an indication of the storyline, but don't give too much away
- include persuasive comments
- include praise for the author.

Check your work carefully and read it aloud to your group.

Activity 3

You will need the Anthology and your writing/drawing materials.

You are going to make a prediction which follows on from the last sentence of the extract you have just read. You may either write a paragraph which describes what happens next, or make a sequence of four drawings to show this. Each drawing should have a caption. You should start by rereading the last three paragraphs of Part One. Check your work and share it with a partner.

Activity 4

You will need the Anthology, Resource Sheet 26, dictionaries, thesauruses and your writing materials.

You are going to continue the collection of verbs of movement. Work in pairs and make a list. If you have time use dictionaries and thesauruses to help you find synonyms and antonyms for the verbs which you have found.

Activity 5

You will need the Anthology.

Work in pairs. You are going to improvise the interview between Lucy and the TV presenter. First discuss which questions could be asked and how Lucy might reply. Then try acting out your ideas with your partner. Present your interview to your group.

Activity 6

You will need Resource Sheet 27 and your writing materials.

Work in pairs. You are going to discuss then write the interview between Lucy and the TV presenter. Think about what has already happened, what Lucy might be asked and how she might reply. Then write a script for this scene. Use the Resource Sheet to help you. You may discuss it together, but you should each write your own copy. Revise and check it, then read your script to your group.

Example:

PRESENTER: When did you first think that something was wrong on the marsh, Lucy?

LUCY: I was coming home from school last week ...

Scheherezade and Bedd Gelert

Activity 1

You will need the Anthology, Resource Sheet 28 and your writing/drawing materials.

You are going to make a cartoon version of the story of Bedd Gelert for younger children. You should talk about the story first in your group and decide what you think the main pictures will be. You will probably need four to six frames to tell the story. Write a short sentence below each picture.

Activity 2

You may need your Anthology for reference. You are going to retell the story of Bedd Gelert or Scheherezade in your group. Each one of you will add one sentence as you go round the group. Try this several times, starting with a different person each time. Discuss the differences between your version and the written one. If there is time, share your story with the class.

Extension: work with a partner. You are going to retell the story in your own words to your partner. Your partner will tell you his or her version of the story at the same time, so you will have to concentrate very hard. Try this several times until your version is clear.

Activity 3

You will need the Anthology and your writing/drawing materials.

In your group, think about and discuss the especially important moments in the story, and choose one. Then work on your own to draw a picture depicting that moment, or continue to work together as a group to plan a "tableau" (a still picture, when you act and "freeze" one moment of the story).

If you do the drawing, decide what you think that the moral or the message of the story could be and write this below the picture. Share your work with the group.

Activity 4

You will need your writing/drawing materials.

Write a modern version of this story where the hero or heroine is misunderstood or unfairly treated. If you prefer you can tell the story in drawings with captions.

Activity 5

You will need the Anthology and your writing materials.

Write a review of one of the stories you have read this week. Refer to the characters, the plot, the theme or moral and any favourite parts, and give your opinion of the story.

Support: use Resource Sheet 23.

Activity 6

You will need the Anthology and your writing materials.

Look at the story of *Scheherezade* and write a different version of the story, told from the King's point of view.

Whichever piece of writing you choose, you should spend time reviewing, editing and proofreading your work. You may want to illustrate it as well.

Myth and Legend

Activity 1

You will need the Anthology, Resource Sheet 29 and your writing materials.

Draw up Circe's action plan for capturing Odysseus' men. You should make sure that each point is clearly set out and listed.

Reread the fifth paragraph first. If you want to, you can use the work from the class discussion to help you start. Check your work and read it to a partner. Can your partner follow it easily?

Activity 2

You will need the Anthology and your writing materials.

Discuss the main points of the story with your group. Then work on your own to write an outline of the story including the main points only. Check your work and read it aloud to a partner to make sure that it is clear.

Activity 3

You will need the Anthology, Resource Sheet 30 and your writing materials.

Read the whole cloze extract carefully. Then write in the missing words. You don't have to remember the original. Other words may fit. Read the whole piece aloud to check it makes sense before you compare it with the original.

Activity 4

You will need the Anthology and your writing/drawing materials.

Reread paragraph 5 in the story of Odysseus and Circe. Notice how it makes you visualise the scene. Then make a series of drawings to show what happened to the men when they entered the palace. Think of a title for your set of drawings. Try to include as many details as you can.

Activity 5

You will need the Anthology, Resource Sheet 31 and your writing materials.

Write a first person account of the fight as if you were the Minotaur. You could do this as a diary extract using Resource Sheet 31. What do you feel? What do you do? Choose verbs which describe your actions and feelings precisely.

Activity 6

You will need the Anthology, Resource Sheet 31 and your writing materials.

Write a first person account from Ariadne's point of view. Write about what you feel and do after you have given Theseus the ball of string. Choose verbs which fit your actions and feelings precisely. You could do this as a diary extract using Resource Sheet 31.

Activity 7

You will need the Anthology, Resource Sheet 31 and your writing materials.

Write a first person account of the fight as if you were Theseus. (You could write a page of his diary.) Think about how you feel as well as what you do. Choose the verbs carefully. For example, "he stabbed" rather than "he hit". You could do this as a diary extract using Resource Sheet 31.

Activity 8

You will need the Anthology and your writing materials.

Retell the story of Theseus and the Minotaur in your own words. Decide which you think are the main scenes and choose your words carefully to help the reader visualise the place, the characters and the action.

Activity 9

You will need the Anthology and your writing materials.

Write a review of your favourite story this week. Explain why you chose this one. Refer to characters, setting, choice of words, action, themes. You may want to illustrate a significant moment from your story.

Italian Recipes

Activity 1

You will need Resource Sheets 20 and 32 and the Anthology. You may also be able to use other books about Italian food, and dictionaries.

On Resource Sheet 20, write down what you already know, using the class list to help you. Then write down what you need to find out. You can work with your group to do this. Use Resource Sheet 32. Work on your own to write sentences about what you have found out. Check them and read them aloud to your group.

Activity 2

You will need the Anthology and your writing materials.

Reread the introduction with your group. Make notes on the food which comes from different areas. Set them out like this:

> The north: polenta, lasagne ....
>
> The south: pizza ....
>
> The forests and foothills: ....
>
> The plains, lakes and hills: ....

Give your work a title and be prepared to report back on one area to your group or the class.

Support: use Resource Sheet 33.

Activity 3

You will need the Anthology and your writing/drawing materials.

You are going to design a poster to persuade people to try Italian food. You should use information from the text, including illustrations. You may start by discussing this with your group, then work on your own. You should add two sentences which would make people want to try Italian food.

Activity 4

You will need the Anthology, Resource Sheet 34 and your writing materials.

You should look carefully at one of the recipes on the Resource Sheet or in the Anthology. Notice how it is set out. Then write down a recipe which you know or make up a recipe of your own. Make sure that your work is set out clearly so that the reader can follow your work easily, for example,

Title

Ingredients (list)

Method

Activity 5

You will need the Anthology, Resource Sheets 20, 32, 35 and 36 and your writing materials.

You are going to use the notes you have made during the week to write a short piece explaining some of the most important points you have learnt about Italian food. You may want to use Resource Sheet 32 to help you organise your information.

Afterwards you may want to write more on your own, referring to other information you found interesting.

Extension: use Resource Sheet 20 to help you to compare and contrast the two books you have been using. Then use the points you have made to help you complete the comparison and contrast frames on Resource Sheets 35 and 36.

Red Riding Hood

Activity 1

You will need the Anthology, Resource Sheet 37 and your writing materials.

You are going to write your own beginning to the story using Resource Sheet 37 to help you. Think about from whose point of view you will write and which details about the setting and character you want to include. Check your work carefully and read it aloud to a partner.

Activity 2

You will need the Anthology, Resource Sheet 38 and your writing materials.

You are going to write your own blurb for a collection of fairy tales, using Resource Sheet 38 to help you. Start by reading the blurb in the Anthology. Decide which tales you would include. Try to choose some adjectives to persuade the reader to try the book. You should check your work and read it aloud to a partner.

Activity 3

You will need the Anthology and your writing materials.

You are going to write an extract from Red Riding Hood's diary, describing her experience.

Extension: retell the whole story from the point of view of the grandmother/the wolf/Red Riding Hood.

Activity 4

You will need the Anthology and your writing/drawing materials.

You are going to design a cover for a version of *Red Riding Hood*. You should decide which important details about the characters and the story you want to include.

Extension: tell the story in three sentences.

Activity 5

You will need the Anthology, Resource Sheet 39 and your writing materials.

Choose one of the scenes from the Resource Sheet. Write a script for this scene. Think about the number of characters, where the scene would be set, etc.

Activity 6

You will need your writing materials.

Plan and draft your own fairy story. Think about the typical features of fairy stories: heroes, villains, a problem, a resolution, a moral or a message.

Landmarks from the Past

Activity 1

You will need the Anthology, Resource Sheet 40 and your writing materials.

Look at the Resource Sheet to see what information you need to explain how people first crossed rivers. Read the paragraphs headed "Fords and bridges" carefully and pick out the information you need to help you to complete the sentences on the Resource Sheet.

Activity 2

You will need the Anthology and your writing materials.

You should look at the picture on page 122 or 123 carefully. Decide on a title which fits this picture, then write some sentences to show what you learn from this picture. Check your sentences and share them with a partner. If you have extra time, choose another picture and do the same.

Extension: make notes on key points from one section of the text. Use these to prepare a short written or oral report for the class, perhaps in a history lesson.

Activity 3

You will need the Anthology, Resource Sheet 41 and your writing materials.

Use the Resource Sheet to help you to find and record information about different periods in history and about huts. Read the questions carefully and skim and scan the text to find the information you need.

Activity 4

You will need the Anthology and your writing materials.

Look carefully at the glossary in Section F and notice how it is organised. Choose five words. Read the definitions. Then write a sentence for each word. This should set the word in context and help to explain what it means.

For example, "the Stone Age boy picked up a sharp flint to defend himself".

Activity 5

You will need the Anthology and your writing materials.

Choose one of the pictures you have discussed during the week. You are going to write as if you were one of the characters below:

- an Iron Age girl or boy living in a hut in Cornwall

- a girl or a boy in the Iron Age village

- a workman building the railway

- a soldier living in one of the hillforts.

You should have some notes from the class writing to help you start. You should use the text and your imagination to write a paragraph, showing this person's thoughts. Edit and proofread your writing and share it with the group.

Poems (2)

Activity 1

You will need the Anthology and your writing materials.

You are going to write six lines to make your own ending to "The Dare".

Line 1 should be one of the friends jeering. It should be set on its own. Lines 2–6 should show the girl's thoughts and what she decides to do.

Keep the lines fairly short. You might try a new line for a new thought. Think about any punctuation you might need.

Check your work and read it aloud to a partner. Use any extra time for redrafting and editing your work.

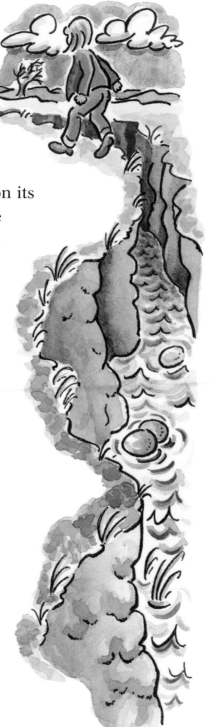

Activity 2

You will need the Anthology and your writing materials.

You are going to write your own haiku about an animal. You will find examples of haiku on pages 136 and 137 of the Anthology. A haiku is a three line poem which gives a picture in words. Line 1 has five syllables, line 2 has seven syllables and line 3 has five syllables.

For example,

Tiger, eyes dark with   (5 syllables)

half remembered forest night   (7 syllables)

stalks an empty cage.   (5 syllables)

Your haiku should aim to give a picture of where the animal is and what it is doing.

Activity 3

You will need the Anthology and your writing materials.

You are going to choose one of the poems for presentation to the class. You should read the poem again and discuss the mood and how you will express it. You should think about how you will change your voices – through pace, pitch and volume. You can also use single and combined voices.

Activity 4

You will need Resource Sheet 42.

Work in pairs. Read the whole poem together. Then discuss which words you think should fill the spaces. Be prepared to justify your choices when deciding on the best fit. Finish by reading the poem aloud to the group and comparing your choices.

Activity 5

You will need the Anthology and your writing materials.

You are going to choose your top three poems from the poems you have read this week. Think carefully about why you choose each one. Then write their titles and several sentences describing the reasons you chose them.

Prepare a reading of your "number one" for your group. Check your writing and make sure that it will be clear to people in your group. Then read the poem aloud and the reasons for choosing it.

The Good Fortunes Gang

Activity 1

You will need the Anthology and your writing materials.

You are going to write a prediction for the next part of the story as if you were Pete. Start by rereading today's extract carefully. Your first sentence should follow on from the last sentence in the extract. Edit and check your work and read it aloud to a partner.

Activity 2

You will need the Anthology and your writing materials.

Work with your group and read aloud the dialogue between Maddy, Toby and Simon in Part One. You should discuss what you know about each of these characters. Then write the name of each character and one thought which each character might have at this point in the story.

Here is an example: TOBY: I wish Maddy didn't pretend to be a health food freak.

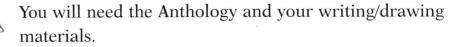

Activity 3

You will need the Anthology and your writing/drawing materials.

Reread the third paragraph of Part One, which describes Simon. Then choose and write one phrase or sentence which stands out. Then make a sketch of Simon which fits the text as closely as possible. Read your sentence to your partner.

Activity 4

You will need the Anthology, writing materials and a dictionary.

Scan the whole text for adverbs and write down five. Then use your dictionary to help you to find the antonyms (opposites) for each adverb. Write these down. Finally, make up a sentence which fits each antonym.

Example:

adverb *snugly* – antonym *uncomfortably*.

The children had to sit uncomfortably on narrow benches.

Activity 5

You will need the Anthology, Resource Sheet 43 and your writing materials.

You are going to write a description of a dream. Write about a real dream if you can remember one, or otherwise make one up. You should try to make your dream as vivid as possible, choosing important details. You should also use at least one simile or metaphor to describe your dream or something in it. For example, "my dream is like a drifting feather". You can use Resource Sheet 43 to help you.

When you have finished, read your work carefully and think about how you could improve it. Do you need to add words? Delete words? Change the order? Have you chosen the best verbs?

Read your work aloud to a partner. You will be given extra time to redraft and perhaps to produce a final version.

Science Fiction
A Fight between Lizards at the Centre of the Earth and The Homecoming

Activity 1

You will need the Anthology and your writing materials.

Read the last paragraph of the section you have just discussed. Then write a prediction which follows on from this and which uses the first person and the present tense. Check your work and share it with a partner.

Extension: write a more extensive prediction from a different point of view.

Activity 2

You will need the Anthology and your writing materials.

Onomatopoeic words imitate the sound they describe.

Examples: splash, crash, hiss, tick, tap, cuckoo, pitter patter

Write a paragraph describing the sounds of a particular place, for example, a zoo or a swimming pool. Include at least five onomatopoeic words.

Activity 3

You will need the Anthology, Resource Sheet 44 and your writing materials.

You should read the whole passage on the Resource Sheet through to yourself. Then, for each space think of a word which fits and write it in the gap. Then, read through the passage with your group, discussing the words you chose. You should be prepared to justify your choice.

Activity 4

You will need the Anthology, Resource Sheet 45 and your writing/drawing materials.

Read the paragraphs on the Resource Sheet carefully and then draw a picture which fits this piece of text. Write a sentence underneath your picture which sums up Harry's feelings.

Extension activity for all groups: read another science fiction story, identifying features of the genre.

Activity 5

You will need the Anthology, Resource Sheet 46 and your writing materials.

You are going to plan a science fiction story and draft the beginning. You may want to look again at the stories in the Anthology to remind yourself of special features of science fiction. For example, strange creatures, other planets, strange places, future settings.

Use Resource Sheet 46 to help you make notes of your own ideas.

Narrative Poetry

Activity 1

You will need the Anthology, Resource Sheet 47 and your writing materials.

Read the cloze version of "The Jumblies" on the Resource Sheet. Find a rhyming word to fit each space. Then compare your version with the original.

Activity 2

You will need Resource Sheets 50 and 51 and your writing materials.

You are going to jot down your thoughts, questions and predictions about the extract of the poem on these Resource Sheets. You could underline any words or phrases you like (sounds, meaning, rhyme) or any stanza which makes you see especially clearly. You could put a question mark by anything you are not sure about. Discuss your thoughts with your group. Be prepared to justify your opinions.

Extension: retell the extract to a younger audience.

Activity 3

You will need Resource Sheets 50 and 51.

You are going to prepare a presentation of the extract of the poem for the class. You should start by rereading silently, then discuss how you are going to present the poem. Decide how many voices you will use for each stanza, for example, 1, 5 and 10 – everyone; individual voices for the other stanzas. Decide how you can vary the pitch (high, low), the volume (loud, soft), the pace (fast, slow) of your voice and what sort of expression you should use.

Mark the text if you need to.

Extension: make a storyboard which shows the sequence of this extract.

Activity 4

You will need the Anthology and your writing/drawing materials.

You should work on your own. Choose one stanza to illustrate. Read the stanza several times. Think about the images and the colours, then make a drawing which fits and give it a title.

Extension: paraphrase the poem in writing.

Activity 5

You will need Resource Sheets 6, 47 to 52 and your writing materials.

You are going to choose the poem which you have liked best this week. Write in more detail about this poem. Explain why you chose it, with reference to the text. Comment on some of the points which have been discussed during the week. For example,

- what it looks like on the page

- unusual language

- rhyme, rhythm.

Edit and check your work. Then **either** prepare a reading of one stanza from the poem **or** draft a few lines using the poem form as your model.

Share your thoughts about the poem with your group.

Seasons of Splendour

Activity 1

You will need the Anthology, Resource Sheet 53 and your writing materials.

You are going to use the frame on Resource Sheet 53 to help you to write an explanatory text about the Indian festival of Holi. You will need to scan the text for information, then write it clearly in your own words. Check your work and share it with the group.

Extension: use the key words from Resource Sheet 53 to write another explanatory text about another subject.

Activity 2

You will need the Anthology and your writing materials.

Use the outline notes you made during the first part of the lesson, or make your own notes, to help you to retell the story so far in your own words. Try to tell the story as clearly and expressively as you can to your partner, then listen carefully while he or she tells you his or her version. Think about the differences between the oral and written versions.

Activity 3

You will need the Anthology and your writing materials.

Read the last section of the story again and then write a prediction which follows on from this. Check your work and then read it aloud to a partner.

Activity 4

You will need the Anthology, Resource Sheet 54 and your writing materials.

Working on your own, read the passage on the Resource Sheet and choose the correct pronoun to fill each gap. Then read through the passage together, discussing the pronouns you all chose. Finally, you could compare your choices with the words in the original story.

Activity 5

You will need the Anthology and your writing/drawing materials.

Read the section where the child Prahlad contradicts the King. Make a drawing of the King to fit this moment in the text. Then write three sentences to describe the King. Check your writing and share it with a partner.

Extension: write a story about a cruel king who is challenged or contradicted by a small child.

Activity 6

You will need the Anthology and your writing materials.

Retell one of the stories you have read this week from a different point of view. For example, tell *The Magic Bowl* from the point of view of the old man's wife. You could start like this:

> My husband came home today with a wonderful surprise.

Activity 7

You will need your writing
materials.

Write your own story about an
object with magic properties. Decide
who your main character is. Decide what the object is,
what it does and how it affects the life of your main
character.

Or

Write a story about a person who is given a special power.
What is the special power? How does the person get this
power? What happens as a result?

Try to include at least one simile or one metaphor, and
one piece of dialogue in your writing.

Edit and proofread it. Then read it aloud to the group.

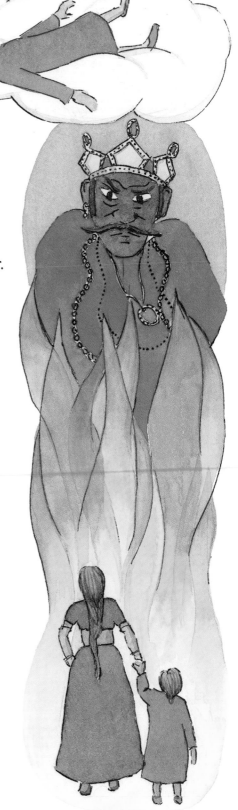

Bible Stories

Activity 1

You will need the Anthology and your writing materials.

Start by rereading the first six paragraphs of "Sentence of Death". Then spend a few minutes with a partner thinking and talking about a time when you did something wrong or told a lie and felt miserable afterwards.

Write a paragraph which describes what you said or did and expresses your feelings clearly. Check your work and read it aloud to the group.

Extension: improvise and then script a scene based on something which has happened or which you imagine, where someone tells a lie and won't admit the truth.

Activity 2

You will need the Anthology and your writing materials.

You should read the first six paragraphs of "Sentence of Death" and then briefly discuss Peter's feelings. Then rewrite this scene as if you were Peter. You could start like this:

> "As I was crouching by the fire a servant asked me if I was a friend of Jesus. I was so scared ...".

Activity 3

You will need Resource Sheet 55, dictionaries and your writing materials.

Read the list of sayings and meanings and then match them up correctly by joining lines. If you have extra time, try using a few of the sayings in your own sentences.

Activity 4

You will need the Anthology and your writing materials.

Read the first scene aloud together. If you are reading what Peter says, show what he is feeling in your voice. Then write all or part of this scene in script form, setting it out clearly in the way shown below.

In the courtyard

SERVANT: Aren't you a friend of the man they've arrested?

PETER: (terrified)   No! No! You've made a mistake!

Activity 5

You will need your writing materials.

You are going to write a short poem about a feeling you have experienced. Try to keep the lines short. Include a simile or metaphor, perhaps at the end. You could use a similar pattern to the poem below. Review your poem carefully and edit and change it if you need to. Then proofread for accuracy. Finally, share your poem with a partner.

I couldn't face

their accusations.

I told a lie.

"I didn't do it!"

They believed me.

I felt

like a rotten apple.

Tornadoes and Hurricanes

Activity 1

You will need the Anthology and your writing materials.

You are going to write a description of a storm, which includes the words listed below. You may find it helps to start by reading either part of the newspaper report, *Isle of Wight Tornado Terror*, or the extract from *The Wizard of Oz*. Your writing should be either an entry for a diary or an extract from a story. Check your writing and read it aloud to a partner.

For example,

> April 21. Woke up this morning to the sound of the wind lashing the trees.

Words to include

> black clouds whirling, smashed to pieces, a swirling tower of wind, danger, whipping, lashed

Activity 2

You will need the Anthology and your writing materials.

Work in pairs. Choose one of the eyewitness accounts in the newspaper report *Isle of Wight Tornado Terror*. Write an interview between the newspaper reporter and this person. Think of the questions the reporter might ask. You may either set your work out as dialogue, using direct speech, or set it out as a script. Check your writing together and read it aloud to your group.

Examples,

"What time was it, PC Bloomfield, when you first realised a dangerous storm was on its way?" asked the reporter.

"Well," replied PC Bloomfield, "It must have been about 11.45 am."

"Where were you at the time?"

Activity 3

You will need the Anthology, a dictionary and your writing materials.

You are going to make a glossary of words connected with storms. Use the text *High Winds*. List the words which are written in bold print. Use the text and a dictionary to help you to write a definition of each word. Check your work carefully.

Activity 4

You will need the Anthology and your drawing materials.

You are going to make a drawing of a storm. This should fit either one part of the description in the report *Isle of Wight Tornado Terror,* or the storm described in *The Wizard of Oz.* One example you could use is the description of what happened to PC Bloomfield. Make sure you read the section of the text carefully first. Make up a caption for your drawing and share it with a partner.

Activity 5

You will need the Anthology and your writing materials.

You are going to use the extract from *The Wizard of Oz* as a basis for a newspaper report on a cyclone. Make sure that the first sentence gives the information: what, where, who and when.

Write in short paragraphs, using the class notes to help you and include an eyewitness comment.

Check your writing and read it aloud to a partner.

The Midnight Fox

Activity 1

You will need the Anthology, Resource Sheet 23 and your writing materials.

You are going to start a reading log to record your first impressions of the story. It will contain:

- questions and thoughts about characters and events

- predictions about how the story will go on and why

- comments on how the story is being told. For example, did the opening get you hooked? Are there any words or phrases or whole sections which made a special impression on you?

- memories and ideas from your own experience which the story has made you think of.

You can use the Resource Sheet to help you. You should work on your own, check your work carefully then read it aloud to your group. Listen carefully to what the other members of your group thought.

Extension: rewrite the scene between Tom and his mother as script.

Or

Script a conversation between Tom's aunt and uncle which shows what they think about Tom.

Activity 2

You will need the Anthology and your writing materials.

Start by talking with your partner about a time when someone asked you to do something you didn't want to. For example, tidy your room, spend time with a relation, swim in deep water, play in a football match. Describe what it was, how you felt and what you did in the end.

You should talk, listen carefully to your partner, then report what he or she said to the group. Did you listen well? Were you accurate?

Or you should write about your experience. When you have finished, check your work carefully and read it aloud to your group.

Activity 3

You will need the Anthology, Resource Sheet 56 and your writing materials.

Use the Resource Sheet to help you to write a three line preposition poem.

Activity 4

You will need the Anthology and your writing materials.

Work in pairs. Take a part each and read aloud the dialogue which starts "I don't want ..." on page 199 and ends "... all the time" on page 200. Try to show what the characters are feeling in your voices.

Then choose one of the characters. Write her/his name. Write two or three sentences to show what you have learned about her or him. Check them carefully and read them aloud to your partner.

Extension: retell Parts One and Two from the point of view of either Tom's mother or father.

Activity 5

You will need the Anthology and your writing materials.

You are going to write your own prediction for the next chapter in the style of the author. You should try to include some of Tom's special ways of using language, for example, comparisons and references to memories.

Activity 6

You will need the Anthology and your writing materials.

You should write your own ending for the story in the style of the author. You should reread the beginning carefully and use the clues there to help you end the story.

Activity 7

You will need the Anthology and your writing materials.

You should write a letter from Tom to Petie. The letter should tell Petie about the fox. You should make sure that you set the letter out clearly in an appropriate way.

Or

Improvise a meeting between Tom and Petie. Imagine that Petie comes to visit Tom at the farm. Think about how they feel, where they go, what they say. You could go on to write the script for this scene.

Or

Improvise a telephone conversation between them when Tom tells Petie about the fox.

Grandpa Chatterji

Activity 1

You will need the Anthology and your writing materials.

You are going to write a letter, as if you were Neetu, to a friend who no longer lives in the area. You should tell her about Grandpa Chatterji and what you feel about him coming to visit. You should use the details in the text as a basis for what you say.

Make sure you set out your letter clearly. Think carefully about how you will begin and end. Look at any examples of letters in your classroom before you start. Check your work and share it with a partner or your group.

Extension: look at other examples of letters, or letters within books, and compare them.

Activity 2

You will need the Anthology and your writing materials.

Start by reading aloud the first three paragraphs of Part One with your group and notice how suspense is built up by using questions. Then imagine a situation where you are waiting at home for a strange new person to arrive. Write in the first person. Your first paragraph should contain some questions as you wonder what this person will be like. Your second paragraph should be shorter and should show the moment when the person arrives.

You could start like this:

> I waited and waited. I pressed my nose against the window pane.

Activity 3

You will need the Anthology and your writing/drawing materials.

You are going to make a close up picture of Grandpa Chatterji, using the words in the text to help you. You should add a thought bubble which contains two or three sentences to show his thoughts at that moment in the story. You could use details from Part One (paragraph beginning "Then there was silence" to "... in a tangle over his brow") or from the last paragraph in Part Three and the first paragraph in Part Four.

Activity 4

You will need the Anthology, Resource Sheet 57 and your writing materials.

Use the text to help you write comparatives for the words on the chart.

Use four of the new words you have formed in sentences.

Activity 5

You will need Resource Sheet 58 and your writing materials.

Reread the last extract. Discuss how the dialogue might continue at the fair. Work alone or with a partner to write a dialogue between Grandpa and Neetu or Grandpa and Sanjay at the fair. Use the Resource Sheet for a starting point and ideas.

Love Letters of Ragie Patel

Activity 1

You will need the Anthology, Resource Sheet 59 and your writing materials.

You are going to work in pairs to plan a script, using the *Love Letters of Ragie Patel* as a model. You will need to decide:

Who? Make a cast list of no more than six characters.

Where? Decide on four scenes in four different places.

When? Which year? Day or night?

What happens? Think of a meeting and an argument.

Use the Resource Sheet to help you to write the first four speeches of your second scene.

Check and read your lines aloud as a group.

Activity 2

You will need the Anthology, Resource Sheet 60 and your writing materials.

Read Ragie's letter again then decide what dad might write in reply. Use the Resource Sheet to draft a short letter from dad, responding to what Ragie has said. Check your writing and share it with a partner.

Activity 3

You will need the Anthology and your writing materials.

Work in pairs and read aloud Scene 1 or a short section from one of the other scenes. Concentrate on showing what your character is like through your voice. Try the scene several times. Then write two sentences about each character.

Activity 4

You will need the Anthology and your writing materials.

Read Scene 1 and the beginning of Scene 2 again, then write from Ragie's point of view, describing what happens when you go into the back lane and meet another boy. This should be written in story form. You could start like this:

> I didn't really want to go outside, but Grandpa made me. I was wandering down the lane when ...

Activity 5

You will need the Anthology, the plan for your script and your writing materials.

You should work in pairs. You are going to write the first one or two scenes of the play you have planned. Each scene should be set in a different place. Check and read it aloud together before you read it to the group. Edit and proofread it.

Bottersnikes and Gumbles

Activity 1

You will need the Anthology and your writing materials.

You are going to rewrite the first section of the story as if you were the King of the Bottersnikes. Remember to use the first person and to show the Bottersnike's point of view. You could start with the sentence below or make up your own.

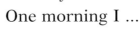

> I am much too sensible to waste my time digging burrows, so I live with my tribe in a rubbish heap. One morning I …

Activity 2

You will need the Anthology, Resource Sheet 61 and your writing materials.

You are going to write a description of the Bottersnike, by completing the description on the Resource Sheet with your own similes. You should try to make your similes as original and as colourful as possible.

Activity 3

You will need Resource Sheets 62 and 63.

First read aloud the passage on Resource Sheet 62 together. Then work on your own to fill in the gaps. When you have finished, reread it and compare your answers with the text on Resource Sheet 63.

PLEASE BE TIDY.

Activity 4

You will need the Anthology, Resource Sheet 64 and your writing materials.

You should work on your own. You are going to write some sentences about Bottersnikes, using the examples on the Resource Sheet as models.

Extension: invent and describe a fantasy being. Include details of habitat, appearance, food and habits. Use at least two similes to make the description clear.

Activity 5

You will need the Anthology and your writing materials.

You are going to write the next chapter of the story. You should write from the point of view of either a Bottersnike or a Gumble or write in the third person. Whichever you choose, remember to plan first:

Who? Gumbles, Bottersnikes – and any new characters?

Where? Down by the creek?

When? Day? Night? ......?

What happens?

What happens in the end?

When you have finished your first draft, check it and read it aloud to your group.

Friends of the Earth

Activity 1

You will need the Anthology and your writing materials.

You are going to write a persuasive statement for each picture on the first three pages of the text. You should use the present tense and make the point that wildlife is under threat, for example, "The barn owls are disappearing".

Check your sentences and read them aloud to your group.

Activity 2

You will need the Anthology, Resource Sheet 65 and your writing materials.

You should use information from the text to support your point of view. Check your sentences and read them aloud to your group.

Activity 3

You will need your writing materials.

Read, copy and complete each of the slogans below.

1. _____ forward to a better future. Join _____ of the Earth.

2. _____ the Howard League today.

3. Sofas to tempt you. Prices _convince _____.

4. Whichever style you choose you can't _____.

5. Adventure sandals. _____ on the wild side.

6. Switch your telephone service to Turquoise and we promise we'll _____ you money.

Now make up a slogan in support of another cause or choose a product you use and make up a slogan to fit. You might also be able to list some other slogans you know.

When you have finished, check your work and read it aloud to your group.

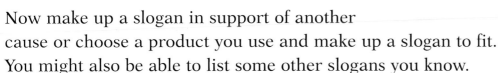

Activity 4

You will need the Anthology and your writing/drawing materials.

You are going to design a poster to persuade people to join Friends of the Earth. You should decide which images to include. You should also invent a slogan. You can choose illustrations from the text if you want to. You should decide on the layout – where you will put the images and the words. Your design will be an outline and you should not expect it to be detailed or perfect at this stage.

Extension: plan, write and script a TV advertisement for a real or imaginary product.

Evaluate the layout and language used in another leaflet or advertisement.

Activity 5

You will need Resource Sheets 65 and 66 and your writing materials.

You will be working on your arguments to support a point of view. Look back at the work you have done on Resource Sheet 65, or devise an argument frame of your own. Organise all your points into order on Resource Sheet 66. Then check your writing and read it aloud to a partner or the group.

Poems (3)

Activity 1

You will need Resource Sheet 67.

You are going to prepare a group reading of "The Listeners" to present to the class. Start by listening to the poem being read again by your teacher. Discuss what sort of mood you want to create by your reading. Decide who will read which lines – one voice, two voices, all voices? Think about how you can make your voices different – soft, loud, high, low, slow, fast. Decide where you will pause. Use and mark the Resource Sheet if you like, to remind yourself what you have decided. Then practise your reading and present it to the class.

Activity 2

You will need Resource Sheet 68 and your writing materials.

Reread the poem from "Midnight Forest" together or on your own. Then use the outline on the Resource Sheet to write your own mystery poem. Think about where it is happening, when it is happening and who is there. Choose your words carefully. Think about meanings and sounds. It doesn't have to rhyme. Make up your own title. Read your poem aloud to a partner, then redraft and revise until you are satisfied.

Activity 3

You will need Resource Sheet 67, which contains a copy of "The Listeners", and your writing/drawing materials.

Talk about the poem with your group, remembering some of the comments from the class discussion. Then use the Resource Sheet to write your own questions about parts of the poem, to mark words you are not sure about or to highlight lines you especially like. Compare your thoughts with those of a partner. Can you answer any of each other's questions? If you have extra time underline words which make you see the scene and draw a picture based on these.

Activity 4

You will need Resource Sheets 67 and 69 and your writing materials.

Read the first eight lines of "The Listeners". Then write your own version of these lines, using the pattern suggested on the Resource Sheet. Read your version to a partner to find out whether it is clear and what it sounds like. Then redraft it and revise it until it is ready to read to your group.

Extension: using Resource Sheet 70, write your own version of the special things poem.

Activity 5

You will need the Anthology, Resource Sheets 67 and 68 and your writing materials.

You are going to choose your favourite two poems from those you have read this week. You should write a paragraph for each poem, recording your thoughts and questions about it and saying why you have chosen it. Check your writing carefully. Share it with a partner. If you have time you could prepare a reading of one of the poems you have chosen.

Extension: make an illustration of one of the poems which reflects something significant about it.

Produce a polished final version of one of the poems written during the week.

Moonfleet

Activity 1

You will need the Anthology, Resource Sheet 71 and your writing/drawing materials.

In your group, read aloud the opening paragraph of the story on Resource Sheet 71. Decide which words give you information about the place and highlight them. Then work on your own to draw a map of the place. Don't forget to give it a title.

Extension: write a poem or prose description about being lonely.

Activity 2

You will need the Anthology and your writing materials.

You should read the last paragraph together and discuss what might happen next. Then write a short prediction which follows on from this paragraph. Try to make it sound as much like John telling the story as possible. Check your work and share it with your group.

Extension: write a first person account of a tense or frightening situation. This might be a true experience or an imaginary one.

Activity 3

You will need the Anthology, Resource Sheet 23 and your writing materials.

You should start a reading log to record your questions, thoughts and comments on the beginning of the story. Include any evidence you can find about the main character, for example, "I think he is imaginative because ...".

You might find it helpful to use Resource Sheet 23.

Activity 4

You will need the Anthology, dictionaries and your writing materials.

Use your dictionary to find definitions of six of the words below. Sometimes words have more than one meaning so be prepared to record several. Write down each word and its definitions. Then write sentences to fit the meanings of three words.

lagoon

precise

parlour

volume

rifle

resolve

descent

tallow

courage

Activity 5

You will need the Anthology and your writing materials.

You should reread the end of the story then write the next section. Try to make your writing sound as much like the original story as possible. Show what John is feeling and try to make your piece exciting and frightening. Check your work carefully.

Activity 6

You will need the Anthology and your writing materials.

You are going to write the beginning of an exciting adventure story about a girl or a boy in an exciting or frightening situation.

You should decide:

who is in your story – not more than three characters

where your story takes place

what happens.

Try to include a description of the place and the characters' feelings. Check your work carefully.

Tom's Midnight Garden

Activity 1

You will need the Anthology, Resource Sheet 72 and your writing materials.

You are going to use the Resource Sheet to write an introduction to a book you have enjoyed, using the introduction to *Tom's Midnight Garden* as a model. You should include:

- title, author

- a sentence which explains why it is one of your favourite books, for example, "I've chosen this as one of my favourite books because ..."

- a short outline of the story, or something important about it

- a final sentence which tells us which episode of the story you have chosen as your favourite part, for example, "Here is ...".

Include some adjectives, with the aim of persuading the reader to read the book, for example, wonderful, fantastic, fascinating.

Activity 2

You will need the Anthology and your writing materials.

You are going to write an entry for Tom's diary. You should reread the story carefully before you start. Think about what Tom does, what he feels, what he sees, and describe the night he goes into the garden. You could start like this:

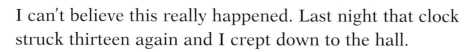

> I can't believe this really happened. Last night that clock struck thirteen again and I crept down to the hall.

Check your writing and read it aloud to a partner.

Activity 3

You will need the Anthology and your writing materials.

You are going to write a prediction which follows on from the last sentence of the extract you have just read. Reread the whole extract carefully first, then carry on telling the story. Try to write in the style of the author. You should aim to write five or six sentences. Check your work and read it aloud to a partner. You might be able to illustrate it if you have extra time.

Activity 4

You will need the Anthology, Resource Sheet 73 and your writing materials.

Read the questions on the Resource Sheet carefully and skim and scan the text to find the information you need to answer them.

Activity 5

You will need the Anthology and your writing/drawing materials.

Choose one of the scenes below:

1. The hall at the beginning of the story

2. The garden as Tom steps onto the doorstep

3. The hall at the beginning of Part Four

Use the details in the text to help you illustrate this scene. Choose a sentence which helps you to see especially clearly and write this under your picture. Then write down one question you have about any part of the story. Read this aloud to a partner and discuss it.

Naturally Wight

Activity 1

You will need the Anthology and your writing/drawing materials.

You are going to design a poster to persuade people to visit the Isle of Wight. You should include pictures, information and a slogan or persuasive sentences. Your poster will be a draft rather than a finished product. Read and compare your slogans or sentences with a partner.

Activity 2

You will need the Anthology, Resource Sheet 74 and your writing materials.

You are going to write an argument which sets out reasons for visiting the Isle of Wight. You should use the frame on Resource Sheet 74 to help you organise your writing. Include more than three points if you need to. Read the text again first. When you have finished share your work with a partner.

Activity 3

You will need the Anthology and Resource Sheet 75.

Read the questions on the Resource Sheet. Scan the text from the beginning up to the heading "Dinosaur Island" for the information you need. Write your answers clearly.

Activity 4

You will need the Anthology, Resource Sheet 76, a dictionary and your writing materials.

Look at the persuasive words on the Resource Sheet. Write their meanings. Then write a context sentence for each word, for example, "One of my models is special".

Extension: write a letter to a tourist information office, asking for specific information about an area.

Activity 5

You will need the Anthology and your writing/drawing materials.

You are going to produce an introductory page for a brochure about either the Isle of Wight, or another area you know, or an imaginary area. You may work on your own or with a partner. You should include:

- an introductory paragraph, which should make your reader want to find out more
- three special features of your place. Give each feature a new paragraph

- a code for behaviour or safety
- other sources of information about your place. These can be real or made up if your place is an imaginary one.

Include any illustrations you need. Check your work and share with your group. You may be given extra time to present a final version.

The Silver Sword and Little House in the Big Woods

Activity 1

You will need the Anthology, Resource Sheet 77 and your writing materials.

Read the part where Ma and Laura meet the bear. Then use the Resource Sheet to rewrite the incident as if you were Ma writing a letter to a friend. You should include what you thought and felt. You should make up an address and a name for Ma's friend. You may want to add a few extra details to make the letter seem like a real one. Check your work and share it with a partner.

Activity 2

You will need the Anthology and your writing materials.

You are going to write a dialogue for the scene when Pa gives Ma and the girls their presents. You should think about how the characters speak in the story and about their feelings. Check that you have used speech marks accurately and set out the dialogue clearly. Then act it out with a partner.

Extension: explore the conflict between Jan and Edek. Write a dialogue or improvise a scene about an argument between them.

Activity 3

You will need, the Anthology, Resource Sheet 23 and your writing materials.

You are going to start a reading log for one of the stories for this week. You can use Resource Sheet 23 to help you. You should record your thoughts about the characters, the storyline and the setting, and any questions and predictions which you have about the story. Check your work and read it to a partner.

Activity 4

You will need the Anthology, Resource Sheet 78 and your writing materials.

Working on your own, read the passage on Resource Sheet 78 and fill in the gaps. Then read through the passage together, discussing the prepositions you chose and deciding which fit best. Finally, compare your work with the extract in the Anthology.

Extension: plan a mime and monologue for the incident when Pa meets the bear.

Activity 5

You will need the Anthology, Resource Sheet 23 and your writing materials.

You are going to write in more detail about one of the stories you have read this week. You should include comments on some or all of the points below, but there may also be other points you want to mention:

- what you like about this story/why you prefer it

- the main characters

- who is telling the story and how this affects you

- the setting

- any exciting or dramatic moments

- differences between the story and your own life

- how you think the story might continue.

Remember to refer to examples from the story to support your opinions.

Check your work and read it aloud to a partner.

Let's Kick Racism out of Football

Activity 1

You will need the Anthology, Resource Sheet 80 and your writing materials.

Use the Resource Sheet to help you argue that racism is still a problem in professional football. Start by scanning the text to find reasons in support of your argument. Check your writing when you have finished and read it aloud to a partner.

Extension: you could write a letter to a local paper to protest about an issue you feel strongly about.

Activity 2

You will need the Anthology and your writing materials.

Look carefully at the pictures and read the captions. Choose five pictures and make up an anti-racism and attention-catching headline to fit each picture. Use key words only, for example, "Top women's footballer scores again".

Check your work and share it with a partner.

Activity 3

You will need the Anthology, Resource Sheet 79 and your writing materials.

Working on your own, read the passage on the Resource Sheet and fill in the gaps using the words at the bottom of the Resource Sheet. You will need to use one word more than once. Then reread the passage aloud with your group, discussing the choices which you made.

Activity 4

You will need the Anthology, your writing materials and a dictionary.

You should use your dictionary to help you write a definition of each word below. Then use each word in a sentence which sets it in context. Check your sentences and share them with a partner.

> incident, ethnic minority, exclude, eliminate, discrimination, harassment, prejudice

Extension: write letters to organisations, asking for information about different issues.

Activity 5

You will need Resource Sheet 65 and your writing materials.

You are going to choose an issue which you feel strongly about. You may already have collected examples during the lesson. You should collect points which support your view using Resource Sheet 65. Write a letter to a newspaper, protesting or complaining about a particular issue. State your point of view and then use the points you have collected to support your argument. You may want to use bullet points or paragraphs to present these points clearly. Think about which words you might use to connect your argument.

Activity 6

You will need Resource Sheet 65 and your writing/drawing materials.

You are going to choose an issue which you feel strongly about. You may already have collected examples during the lesson. You should collect points which support your view using Resource Sheet 65. Make a poster to inform people about the issue and to persuade them to consider your point of view. You should include a statement and pieces of supporting information. You can include drawings as well as writing.

You should check your work carefully. Ask your group to help you evaluate how clear, informative and persuasive your writing is.

Poems (4)

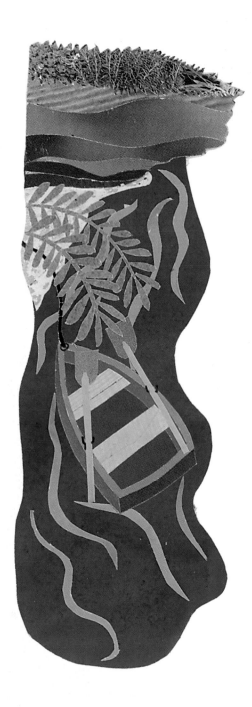

Activity 1

You will need the Anthology and your writing materials.

Read the extract from "The Prelude" again. Imagine that you are on holiday in a beautiful place in the mountains. Write a postcard to a friend at home, telling him or her about the evening when you went out on your own in the boat on the lake. What did you see? What did you hear? What did you feel? You may use the sentence below as a starter if you wish. Check your work and share it with a partner.

> "We're staying by a lake in the mountains. Yesterday I ..."

Extension: read other poems and think about the similarities and differences between the poems you have read. Which do you prefer, and why?

Activity 2

You will need the Anthology.

You are going to work with your group to prepare a reading of either the first or the second page of the extract from "The Prelude". Read the whole of this part on your own. Then discuss which lines can be read together and which can be read individually. Think carefully about the punctuation and where you need to pause. Remember that you can vary your voice by changing the pace, the pitch and the volume. Practise your reading, then present it to another group or to the class.

Activity 3

You will need the Anthology, your writing materials and a dictionary.

You are going to prepare a glossary to help a younger child understand the poem. You should choose at least five unfamiliar words and use a dictionary to help you write the meanings. Work on your own, but share your definitions with a partner.

Activity 4

You will need the Anthology and your writing/drawing materials.

Choose one of the poems, "Stopping by Woods on a Snowy Evening" or "The Prelude" (the first eleven lines). Read it through carefully and make sure that you understand the details. Think about what the words make you see. Then make a drawing which fits the poem/extract as closely as possible. Make up a sentence which says something important about your drawing and write it underneath.

Extension: think of a place which made a special impression on you. Write a description of the place and how you felt, or draw a picture of it.